Editor
Lorin Klistoff, M.A.

Managing Editor
Karen Goldfluss, M.S. Ed.

Editor-in-Chief
Sharon Coan, M.S. Ed.

Illustrators
Wendy Chang
Ana Castanares
Agi Palinay

Cover Artist
Barb Lorseyedi

Art Coordinator
Kevin Barnes

Imaging
Alfred Lau
James Edward Grace

Product Manager
Phil Garcia

Publisher
Mary D. Smith, M.S. Ed.

Written and Compiled by

J.L. Smith

Teacher Created Resources, Inc.
6421 Industry Way
Westminster, CA 92683
www.teachercreated.com
ISBN: 978-0-7439-3308-7
©2002 Teacher Created Resources, Inc.
Reprinted, 2011
Made in U.S.A.

Table of Contents

Introduction

The old adage, practice makes perfect, can really hold true for your child and his or her education. The more practice and exposure your child has with concepts being taught in school, the more success he or she is likely to find. For many parents, knowing how to help their children can be frustrating because the resources may not be readily available.

As a parent it is also difficult to know where to focus your efforts so that the extra practice your child receives at home supports what he or she is learning in school.

This book has been designed to help parents and teachers reinforce basic skills with their children. *Practice Makes Perfect* reviews basic math skills for children in kindergarten. The math focus is on numbers and patterns. While it would be impossible to include in this book all concepts taught in kindergarten, the following basic objectives are reinforced through practice exercises. These objectives support math standards established on a district, state, or national level. (Refer to Table of Contents for the specific objectives of each practice page.)

- Tracing numbers 1–10
- Working with numbers 0–10
- Matching numbers to objects
- Counting shapes and objects
- Matching number names
- Estimating and comparing groups

- Drawing objects to match numerals
- Matching equal groups
- Sequencing numbers
- Drawing shape, color, and object patterns
- Writing letter and number patterns
- Creating patterns

There are 41 practice pages organized sequentially, so children can build their knowledge from more basic skills to higher-level math skills. Following the practice pages, there is an answer key.

How to Make the Most of This Book

Here are some useful ideas for optimizing the practice pages in this book:

- Set aside a specific place in your home to work on the practice pages. Keep it neat and tidy with materials on hand.

- Set up a certain time of the day to work on the practice pages. This will establish consistency. An alternative is to look for times in your day or week that are less hectic and conducive to practicing skills.

- Keep all practice sessions with your child positive and constructive. If the mood becomes tense, or you and your child are frustrated, set the book aside and look for another time to practice with your child. Forcing your child to perform will not help. Do no use this book as a punishment.

- Help with the instructions, if necessary. If your child is having difficulty understanding what to do or how to get started, work the first problem through with him or her.

- Review the work your child has done. This serves as reinforcement and provides further practice.

- Allow your child to use whatever writing instruments he or she prefers. For example, colored pencils can add variety and pleasure to drill work.

- Pay attention to the areas in which your child has the most difficulty. Provide extra guidance and exercises in those areas. Allowing children to use drawings and manipulatives, such as coins, tiles, game markers, or flash cards, can help them grasp difficult concepts more easily.

- Look for ways to make real-life application to the skills being reinforced.

Practice 1

1 1 1 1 1   6 6 6 6

2 2 2 2 2   7 7 7 7

3 3 3 3 3   8 8 8 8

4 4 4 4 4   9 9 9 9

5 5 5 5   1 0 1 0 1 0

Practice 2

O

O

zero

zero

Practice 3

|
|

one

one

Practice 4

2

2

two

two

Practice 5

3

3

three

three

Practice 6

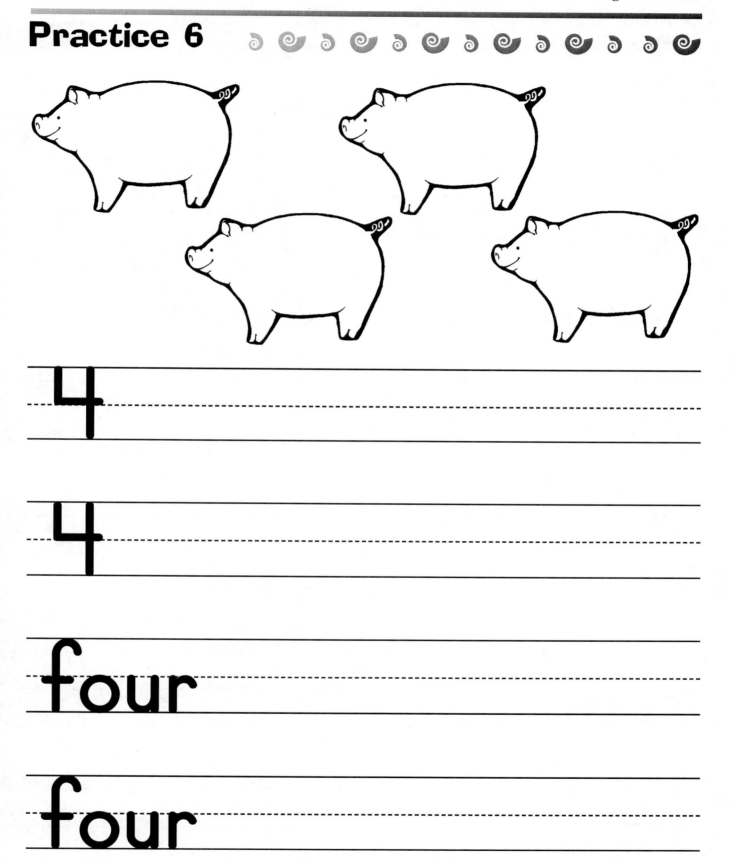

4

4

four

four

Practice 7

5

5

five

five

Practice 8

6

6

six

six

Practice 9

7

7

seven

seven

Practice 10

8

8

eight

eight

Practice 11

q

q

nine

nine

Practice 12

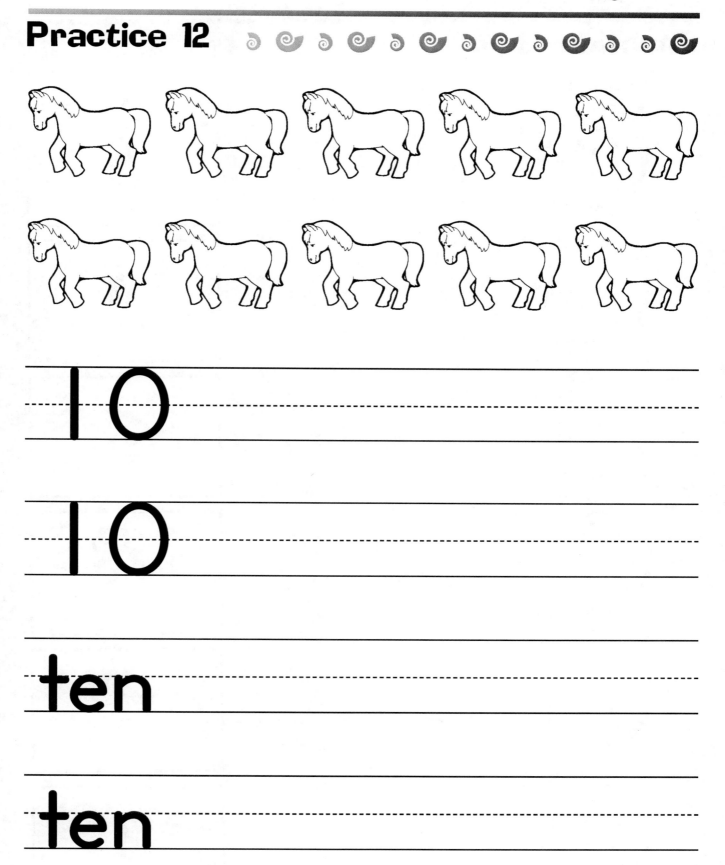

10

10

ten

ten

Practice 13

Draw a line from each balloon to its matching number.

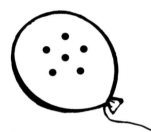

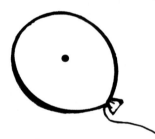

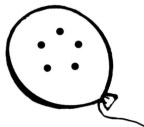

5
2
3
6
1
4

Practice 14

Count the number of things on each shelf of the food cart. Draw a line to the numeral that matches. Color the picture.

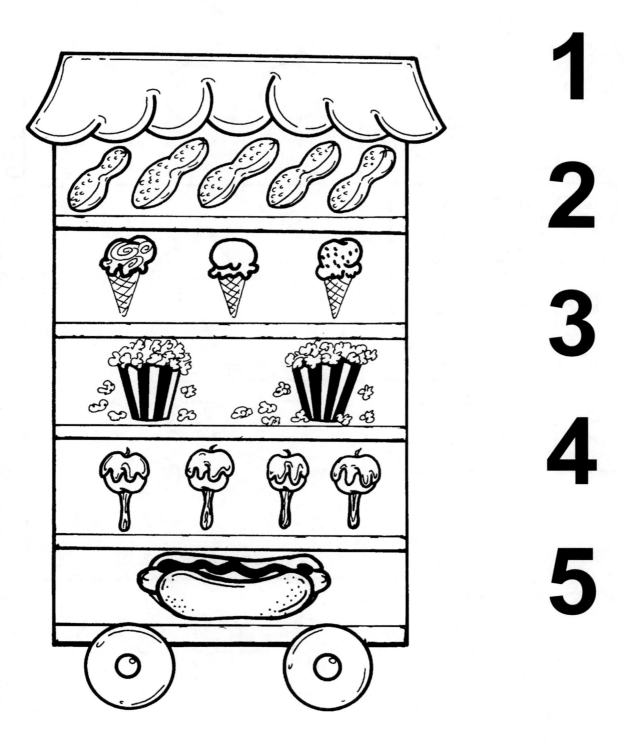

1

2

3

4

5

Practice 15

How many?

   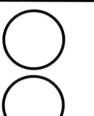 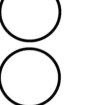 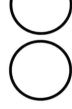

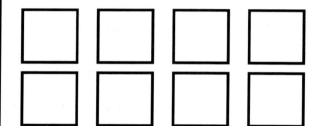 

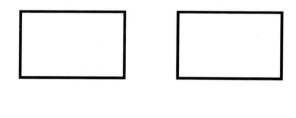 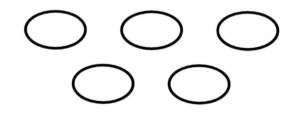

 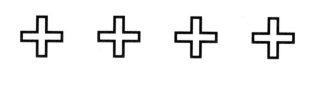

Practice 16

Match the names to the numbers.

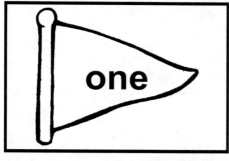 

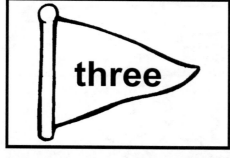 

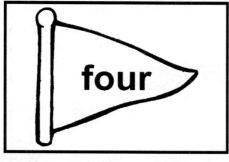 

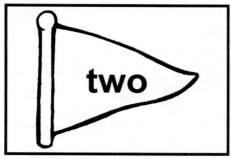 

Practice 17

Directions: Count the objects. Write the correct number in each box.

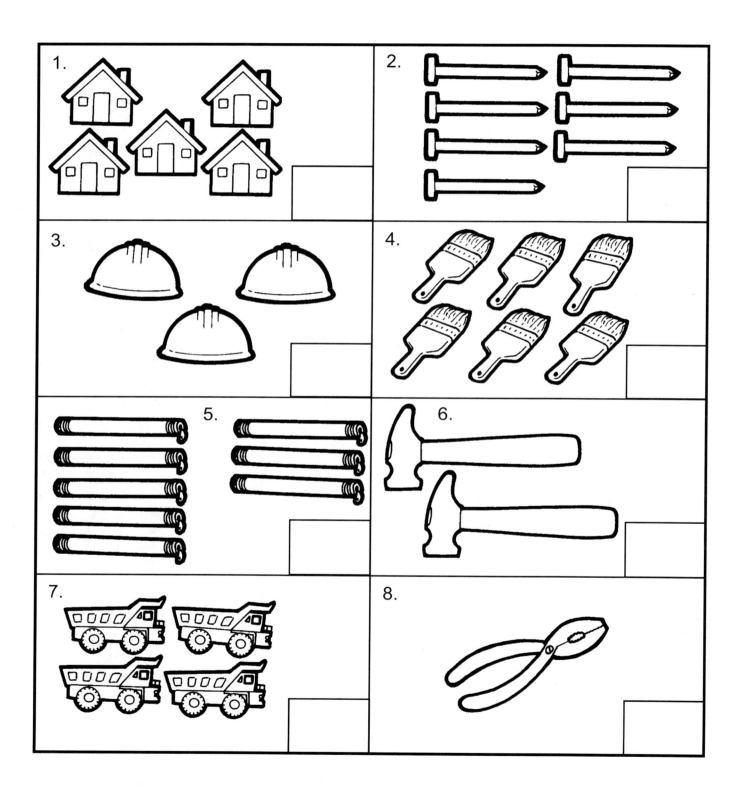

Practice 18

Directions: Write the correct numeral in each box.

1.

2.

3.

4.

5.

6.

Practice 19

Circle the numeral that tells how many.

	1	2	3			3	4	5
	2	3	4			2	3	4
	3	4	5			3	4	5
	1	2	3			1	2	3
	1	2	3			0	1	2

Practice 20

1. Count the snowflakes.

2. Write the number in the box at the bottom of the page.

3. Color.

How many snowflakes?

Practice 21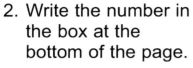

1. Count the bees.

2. Write the number in the box at the bottom of the page.

3. Color.

How many bees?

Practice 22

1. Count the people on or near the bus.
2. Write the number in the box.

Practice 23

Circle the group that has fewer things in it.

1.

2.

3.

4.

5.

6.

7.

8.

Practice 24

Circle the group that has more things in it.

1.

2.

3.

4.

5.

6.

7.

8.

Practice 25

Estimate how many are in each group. Write your estimate. Then count the items in each group. Write the true number.

1.

Estimate _____

Number _____

2.

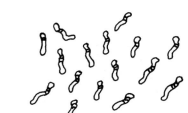

Estimate _____

Number _____

3.

Estimate _____

Number _____

4.

Estimate _____

Number _____

5.

Estimate _____

Number _____

6.

Estimate _____

Number _____

7.

Estimate _____

Number _____

8.

Estimate _____

Number _____

Practice 26

Draw buttons on the snowmen. Use the number to tell you how many buttons to draw.

Practice 27

Draw apples on the trees. Use the number on the tree to tell you how many apples to draw.

Practice 28

Match sets that have the same number in them. Draw a line to equal groups.

1.

2.

3.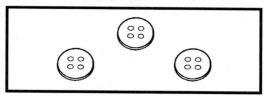

4.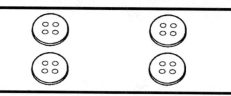

5.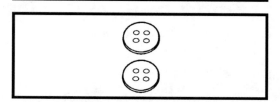

6.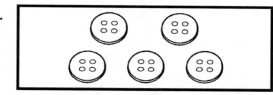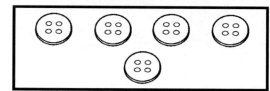

7.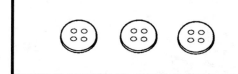

8.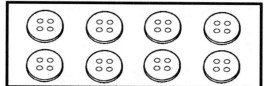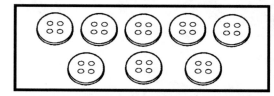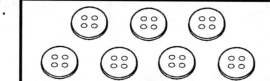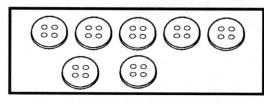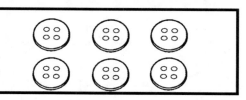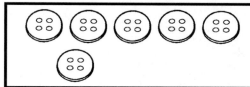

#3308 Practice Makes Perfect: Numbers and Patterns   **31**

Practice 29

Draw a line between the groups that have the same number of items in them.

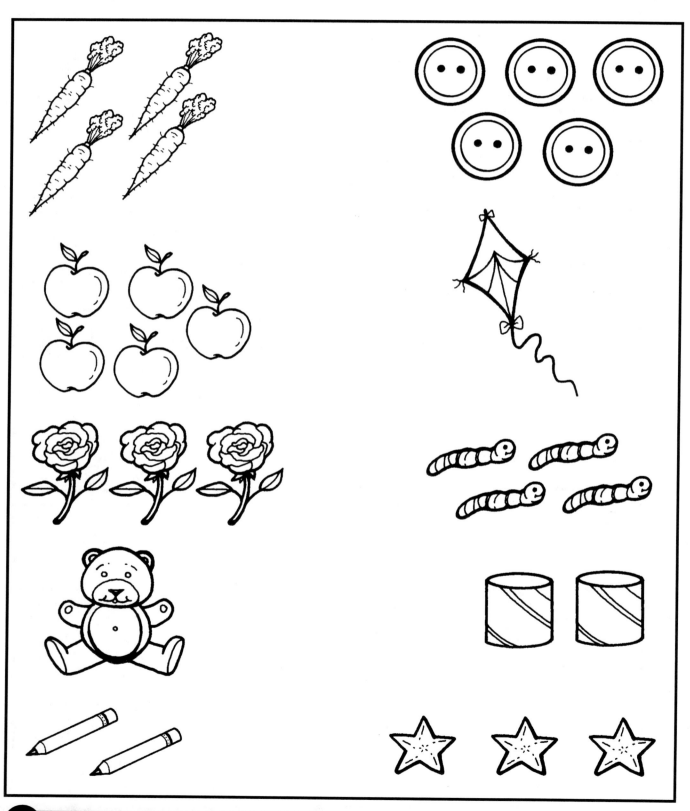

Practice 30

Draw a line to match the same numbers.

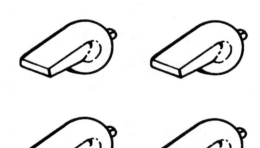

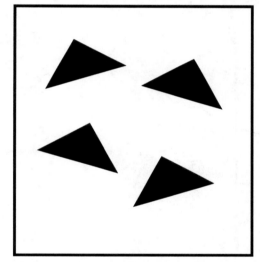

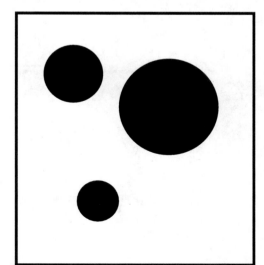

Practice 31

The bears are on parade today. Some of them have lost their numbers. Help them get in order by writing the correct number under each one.

1   2   ___   4   5

10   9   ___   ___   6

11   ___   13   14   ___

20   ___   18   ___   16

Practice 32

To find out who won the race, connect the dots from 1–12. Color the picture.

Practice 33

Follow the dots fo finish the picture.

Practice 34

Write the numerals from 1 to 100.

1	2	3				7	8	9	
11			14	15	16	17		19	20
21			25		27	28	29	30
31		33	34		36			39	
41		43			46	47		49	50
	52	53		55		57		59	
61	62		64		66		68		70
71		73	74		76	77		79	80
81		83			86		88	89	90
91		93	94			97	98		100

Practice 35

Draw the next thing in each series.

1. 	
2. 	
3. 	
4. 	
5. 	

Practice 36

Draw a shape to finish the pattern.

Practice 37

Continue each pattern.

Color the beads.

1. 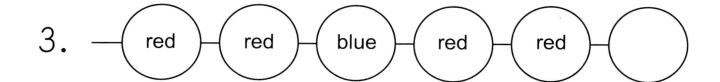 blue — green — blue — green — blue — ( )

2. 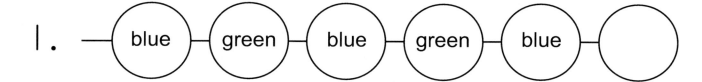 orange — purple — orange — purple — orange — ( )

3. 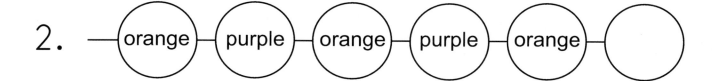 red — red — blue — red — red — ( )

4. 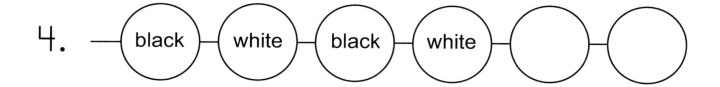 black — white — black — white — ( ) — ( )

5. brown — yellow — yellow — brown — yellow — ( )

6. 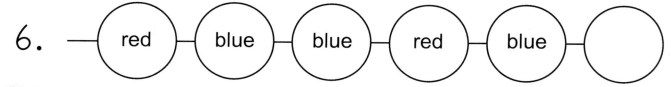 red — blue — blue — red — blue — ( )

Practice 38

Continue each pattern by drawing what comes next.

1.

   _____ _____ _____

2. _____ _____ _____

3. _____ _____ _____

4. _____ _____ _____

5. _____ _____ _____

6. _____ _____ _____

Practice 39

Write the next letter or number in each series.

1. A B A B A B A B _____

2. A A B A A B A A _____

3. A B B A B B A B _____

4. 1 2 1 2 1 2 1 _____

5. X X X Y X X X Y X X X _____

6. 1 2 2 1 2 2 1 2 _____

7. A B C A B C A B _____

Practice 40

Write the next number in each series.

A. 1, 2, 3, 4, 5, 6, 7, 8, _____

B. 2, 4, 6, 8, 10, 12, 14, 16, _____

C. 1, 3, 5, 7, 9, 11, 13, 15, _____

D. 5, 10, 15, 20, 25, 30, 35, 40, _____

E. 10, 20, 30, 40, 50, 60, 70, 80, _____

F. 9, 8, 7, 6, 5, 4, 3, 2, _____

G. 1, 1, 2, 2, 3, 3, 4, 4, 5, 5, _____

H. 1, 4, 7, 10, 13, 16, _____

I. 1 2 3, 1 2 3, 1 2 _____

J. 1 2 2, 1 2 2, 1 2 _____

K. 1, 2 2, 3 3 3, 4 4 4 _____

L. 1 1 2, 1 1 3, 1 1 2, _____

Practice 41

Choose a pattern of color for the tie on the left. Create a pattern on the tie on the right. Color the patterns.

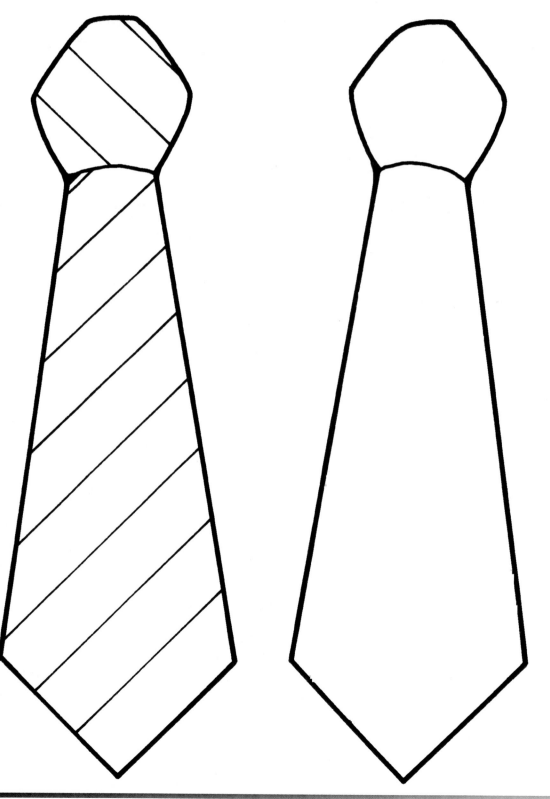

Answer Key

Page 4
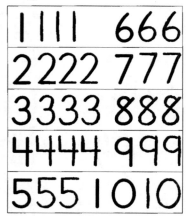

Page 16

Page 17
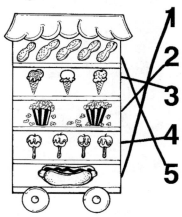

Page 18
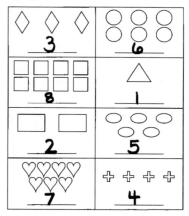

Page 19
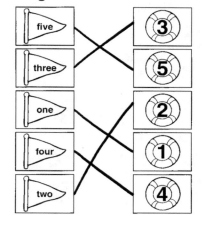

Page 20
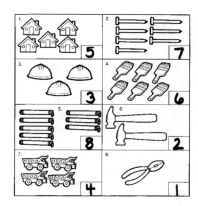

Page 21
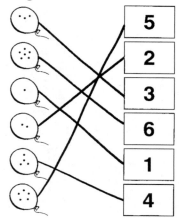

Page 22
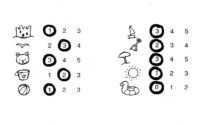

Page 23

Answer Key

Page 24

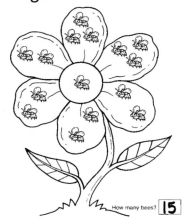

How many bees? 15

Page 25

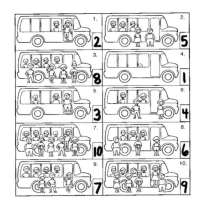

Page 26

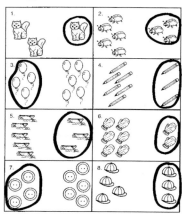

Page 27

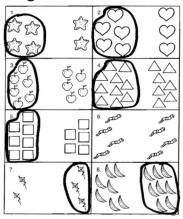

Page 28

1. Estimate **Answers will vary.** Number **10**
2. Estimate **Answers will vary.** Number **16**
3. Estimate **Answers will vary.** Number **20**
4. Estimate **Answers will vary.** Number **12**
5. Estimate **Answers will vary.** Number **5**
6. Estimate **Answers will vary.** Number **25**
7. Estimate **Answers will vary.** Number **7**
8. Estimate _____ Number **1**

Page 29

Page 30

Page 31

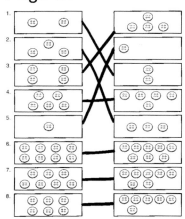

Page 32

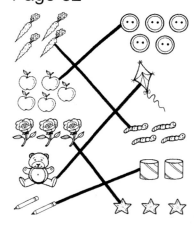

Answer Key

Page 33

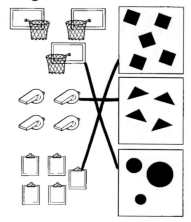

Page 34

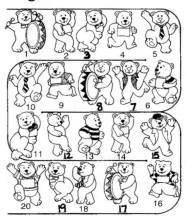

Page 35

Page 36

Page 37

Page 38

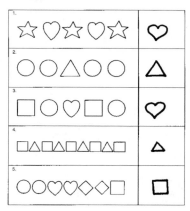

Page 39

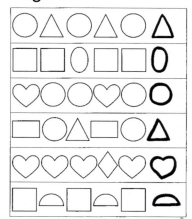

Page 40

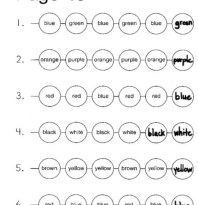

1. blue – green – blue – green – blue – **green**
2. orange – purple – orange – purple – orange – **purple**
3. red – red – blue – red – red – **blue**
4. black – white – black – white – **black** – **white**
5. brown – yellow – yellow – brown – yellow – **yellow**
6. red – blue – blue – red – blue – **blue**

Page 41

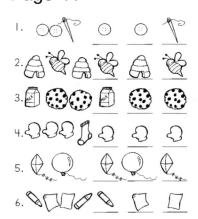

Answer Key

Page 42

1. A B A B A B A B   __A__
2. A A B A A B A A   __B__
3. A B B A B B A B   __B__
4. 1 2 1 2 1 2 1   __2__
5. X X X Y X X X Y X X X   __Y__
6. 1 2 2 1 2 2 1 2   __2__
7. A B C A B C A B   __C__

Page 43

A. 1, 2, 3, 4, 5, 6, 7, 8,	__9__
B. 2, 4, 6, 8, 10, 12, 14, 16,	__18__
C. 1, 3, 5, 7, 9, 11, 13, 15,	__17__
D. 5, 10, 15, 20, 25, 30, 35, 40,	__45__
E. 10, 20, 30, 40, 50, 60, 70, 80,	__90__
F. 9, 8, 7, 6, 5, 4, 3, 2,	__1__
G. 1, 1, 2, 2, 3, 3, 4, 4, 5, 5,	__6__
H. 1, 4, 7, 10, 13, 16,	__19__
I. 1 2 3, 1 2 3, 1 2	__3__
J. 1 2 2, 1 2 2, 1 2	__2__
K. 1, 2 2, 3 3 3, 4 4 4	__4__
L. 1 1 2, 1 1 3, 1 1 2,	__113__

Page 44

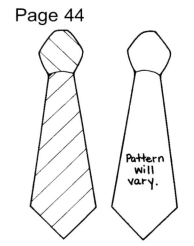

Pattern will vary.

